# SEXY

## Doesn't Have A Dress Size

### ...Lessons in Love

by

Parry "Ebony Satin" Brown

Published and distributed by:
ShanKrys Publishing, Inc.
1525 Aviation Boulevard, Ste A106
Redondo Beach, California 90278-2800
(310) 213-2515
Fax (310) 514-1399
parnelle.com
shankryspublshng@aol.com

First Printing, February 1999

*Second Edition:* First printing, March 2000
This printing, June 2000

10 9 8 7 6 5 4 3 2

*Cover Design*

Lexus Graphics
Redondo Beach, California
(310) 370-0234

*Cover Illustration*

Juanita Howard
Houston, Texas
Jhowardart@aol.com

# Table of Contents

## Dedicated to all the wonderful women in my life!

*To those who walked before me..*

**Mama** *...thank you for all that you have given me. I miss you so much. You were so right, the best was yet to come!*

*To those that walk beside me...*

**Mary, Lorraine, Jackie,** and **Beatrice** *...Being your sister is everything to me.*

*To those who walk with me...*

**Glynda, Blanche, Portia, Victoria, Rosie, Twania, Wanda, Mona,** and **Rico** *...friends are the part of heaven that God has put on earth.*

*To those who walk behind me...*

**Nicolle, Michelle, Shanelle, Krystal** and **Kendra** *(RIP 1998) ...you fill my heart and life with love*

*To those who struggle with me...*

My **Sistahgurlfriends** who recognize the need for change and are willing to do whatever it takes to afford that change.

# From The Heart

First and foremost I give thanks to my Lord and Savior, Jesus Christ. To God the Father for so richly blessing me with the talent of the written and spoken word. For without Them none of this would be possible.

When a friend called me three years ago and asked me to facilitate a seminar I was surprised. She told me that I motivated her every time we spoke and that I was a natural. That withstanding I was still scared to death. But with God as my co-pilot I did it and today I am helping women to change their lives from coast to coast. Thank you, *Rico*. You opened the door and I boldly walked through it.

Thank you *Nicolle* for choosing me as your mother. I don't know what I would have done without your phone calls while on the road *Michelle*. You have made the journey bearable. *Mary* you believed in me enough to have my back, you are truly a rare and wonderful sister. My dear friend *Glynda* who is the keeper of my dream and friend that has always been there for a Sistahgurlfriend. To my new and wonderful love *Neville*, thank you for making my heart sing.

*Victoria, Rosie, Lloyd, Denise, Jo Emily, Wanda, Tangy, Sam & the Boys* kept a lookout for a sistah constantly while I was on the road. Encouraging me every step of the way. Thank you seems so inadequate.

# Life's Enrichment

Author Unknown

The highest aim in life - *To know God and do His Will!*
The most enriching good habit - *Complimenting others*
The most destructive bad habit - *Worry*
The greatest joy - *Giving*
The greatest loss - *Loss of self-respect*
The most satisfying work - *Helping others*
The ugliest endangered species - *Dedicated leaders*
Our greatest natural resource - *Our youth*
The ugliest look - *A frown*
The greatest "shot in the arm" - *Encouragement*
The greatest problem to overcome - *Fear*
The most effective sleeping pill - *Peace of mind*
The most crippling failure disease - *Excuses*
The surest way to limit God - *Unbelief*
The most powerful force in life - *Love*
The most dangerous piranha - *A gossiper*
The greatest Life-Giver - *The Creator*
The worlds most incredible computer - *The brain*
The worst thing to be without - *Hope*
The deadliest weapon - *The tongue*
The two most power-filled words - *"I Can"*
The greatest asset - *Faith*
The most worthless emotion - *Self-pity*
The most beautiful attire - *A SMILE!*
The most prized possession - *Self esteem*
The most powerful channel of communication - *Prayer*
The most contagious spirit - *Enthusiasm*
The most urgent need - *SALVATION*
The greatest attribute of Jesus - *Obedience*
The GREATEST - *GOD*

# *The Difference Between Strength and Courage*
~Author Unknown~

It takes strength to be firm,
It takes courage to be gentle.

It takes strength to stand guard,
It takes courage to let down your guard.

It takes strength to conquer,
It takes courage to surrender.

It takes strength to be certain,
It takes courage to have doubt.

It takes strength to fit in,
It takes courage to stand out.

It takes strength to feel a friend's pain,
It takes courage to feel your own pain.

It takes strength to hide your own pains,
It takes courage to show them.

It takes strength to endure abuse,
It takes courage to stop it.

It takes strength to stand alone,
It takes courage to lean on another.

It takes strength to love,
It takes courage to be loved.

It takes strength to survive,
It takes courage to live.

May the world hug you today
With its warmth and love and, may the wind carry a voice

That tells you there is a friend
Sitting in another corner of the world wishing you well!

# *Preface*

On the pages that follow I will deal with the truth about self esteem and self acceptance as I see it. While I am not an expert in physiology or psychology, I *am* an expert on living life as a woman who has won the self esteem battle.

You see, when I was born I was a size 12. (Poor Mama!). I spent forty years trying to fit the mold of what everyone else told me I should be. But one morning God mercifully splashed cold water in my face and I realized He didn't make an inferior product. And please make no mistake about it, I am truly made in God's image.

What I share in this book are my experiences and my insight. Use what you can and discount the rest. My prayer is that just one sentence in this booklet will cause you to pause. Pause and accept just one thing about yourself that you have toiled with most, if not *all*, of your life. That will be the beginning of your change!

The questions contained on the pages that follow have no right or wrong answers. It is an exercise to cause you to think about where your life is verses where you want it to be.

The questions following each chapter are in two parts: *Now* and *In 90 Days*. The *Now* questions are intended to be completed in the seminar setting or immediately thereafter. The *In 90 Days* questions are to be completed after 90 days of putting the learned principles into place.

Change will only come if you desire it and there is no magic or quick fix to increasing self esteem. It will take courage and strength on a daily basis to overcome some of the issues we have dealt with since infancy.

The *Sexy Doesn't Have a Dress Size Seminar Series* is meant to help us with some of these issues and most of all to let us know we are not alone in our constant struggles.

Like pills in a bottle that do you no good if not taken, the questions set forth here will do you no good if not answered honestly. The most important element of any behavioral modification is the willingness to change.

I wish you love, peace of mind and a confidence that shines like the great North Star!

# *Love Don't Love Nobody*

For more years than I care to count when I looked in the mirror, no one looked back at me. How is that possible, you ask? Oh, I saw what I needed to see... I didn't have a cowlick, spinach in my teeth, or crust in my eyes. But those eyes never looked back at me. They were too busy looking for someone else to love me.

You see, I didn't love that woman who looked back at me in the mirror, and even worse I didn't see any thing worth loving. I didn't realize then if I didn't love her, no one else would. Why should they? I sought love from every where and everyone, except in the mirror.

I never wanted to make anyone angry because they wouldn't love me. I was looking for love in all the wrong places. I was looking for love for the sake of saying someone loved me. I would have betrothed my very soul if I thought I would have received love and acceptance in return.

Well, SISTAHGURLFRIENDS, love don't love nobody, not even you! YOU have to love you! You have to look deep inside to find just one thing that you adore about yourself and stop waiting for others to find it. Do you have any idea why others don't find things they adore about you? They ain't lookin' for it!

The lesson for this first chapter is the most important of them all. Once you have made the life altering discovery that loving you begins with YOU, find a mirror, look in it, REALLY look in it...and find something on the outside you really like! Okay, so maybe really like is pushing it....find something that is not half bad!

Now comes the hard part...Say it out loud! It's OK, there is no one there but you. Say it!
*"My hair sure does shine pretty."*
*"My eyes sparkle when I smile."*
*"This lipstick sure makes my teeth look white."*

You get the idea. You must do this every day. Even if you say the same thing everyday for a week or a month, a quarter, or a year. Keep saying it out loud.

Once you really believe it, find another part of your outward appearance you really like. Repeat this exercise until the woman in the mirror finally starts to look back at you. Do it until she smiles when you says good morning. Do it until she says I love you and really means it!

It is a nice reward when others love us, but the absolute treasure is when we love ourselves!

# Lesson One (Now)

1.   When you look in the mirror what do you see?

2.   Do you smile at yourself in the mirror?

3.   What do you like most about your body?

4.   What do you like least about your body?

5.   What would you like to change about your body?

6.   What do you need to do to accomplish this?

7.   When is the last time you told someone you love them?

8.   When is the last time you told yourself 'I love you'?

# *Notes*

# Lesson One (In 90 Days)

1.  When you look in the mirror what do you see?

2.  Do you smile at yourself in the mirror?

3.  What do you like most about your body?

4.  What do you like least about your body?

5.  What would you like to change about your body?

6.  What do you need to do to accomplish this?

7.  When is the last time you told someone you love them?

8.  When is the last time you told yourself 'I love you'?

# *Notes*

# I Ain't Ugly

How in the world do we get to this not so pleasant place in our lives? A place where we don't want to be and then can't understand why others don't want to join us there.

For me, it was my childhood. I grew up in a family where dark skin wasn't in. You see, my grandfather was as dark as the rich soil he toiled as a poor farmer and my grandmother could have been of European decent. So their offspring was the rainbow coalition for sure. Being caught up in the light is right fallacy that still plaques African Americans going into the new millennium, I bought into the myth that I couldn't be dark and pretty.

I descend from a long line of people of size, however, the outside world is not so accepting. Being a fat child is no day on a Carribean Beach. Now read carefully here -- at home I am 'dark and ugly' and at school I am fat. Oh yeah, I forgot to mention I wore VERY thick glasses . LAWDHAMURCY this poor child had no refuge and no self esteem!

I think you are getting the picture! So I lived the first eighteen years of my life believing that I wasn't pretty and no man would ever want me because I was 'dark, ugly and fat' (and my aunt also told me this on a regular basis).

Then, Mr. Brown came along, smiled at me and I married him. He was (and still is) a very attractive man who wanted, with very little investment on his part, a woman who would be willing to give him 100%. I was more than happy to give 200% because after all, I was lucky to have found any man with a blood pressure willing to have me.

His family was the poster people for Slim Fast. So now I am married to a man who also thinks I am fat and missed no opportunity to tell me. This unacceptable behavior went on for twenty-two years. Yes, I said 22!

Remember earlier I said God was merciful and gave me a wake up call? Well, SISTAHGURLFRIEND, I wish I could say that one morning I woke up and I thought I was all that, but nothing worth having is ever that easy.

In this chapter our lesson is a difficult one. You must take those most important steps on the long road to a healthy self love – admit that something or someone got you to this point. Forgive them and then forgive yourself. Now move forward.

No healing can take place without forgiveness. And forgiving ourselves is the most difficult. Forgive yourself for allowing others in influence your feelings about YOU. Seek your spiritual higher power and rely on it daily...on second thought, make that moment by moment.

The woman that I look at in the mirror each morning and tell her I love her took days, weeks, months, and years to come into being. But now when I stand before that mirror I know she is beautiful inside and out.

She is not thin (don't wanna be anymore)! She is deep rich chocolate brown with strawberry dipped red lips a smile that could light up a city block, eyes that are warm, expressive and caring, and a personality that invites people to come on by and sit a spell!

*Parry 'EbonySatin' Brown*

# Lesson Two (Now)

1.  As a child did someone say negative things to or about you? What were they?

2.  How did it make you feel?

3.  How did you see yourself as a child?

4.  How do you see yourself now?

5.  Are you consumed with the desire to change your appearance?

6.  What reward(s) are you putting on hold until you change your appearance?

7.  Are you staying in relationships with people because you are lucky they are with you?

8.  Do you allow people to use you?

# *Notes*

# Lesson Two (In 90 Days)

1. Have you begun to work toward forgiveness of those who had a negative influence on you?

2. How does forgiving others make you feel?

3. Are you making progress in forgiving yourself for allowing others to mistreat you?

4. How do you feel about yourself and those people now?

5. Are you consumed with the desire to change your appearance?

6. What reward are you putting on hold until you change your appearance?

7. Are people treating you differently since you are making changes?

8. Is NO a complete sentence?

# *Notes*

# *Celebration*

Have you ever been in the presence of someone who makes you feel like they are doing you a favor by being with you? SISTAHGURLFRIEND, you know what I am talking about! There are those people who mask their own insecurities by making sure you don't feel too good about the person that you are!

There are those who would rather walk on broken glass than tell you they are proud of you for getting that promotion, or that you look fantastic in that new suit. They make you think you are lucky that they want to be in your presence or are paying you any attention. They tolerate you, while you celebrate them.

Now I say to you, would you rather be tolerated or celebrated? I choose celebration. I want to surround myself with people who want to be in my aura. People who laugh with me, instead of at me. People who give me back as much or more than I am giving them. People who are happy to see me succeed! People who are secure enough in themselves to be able to compliment me on the small successes like having a good hair day. And know they can expect the same in return.

I want to be in the circle where people are constantly improving themselves so that my improvements will not draw envy!

Surround yourself with Sistahgurlfriends who have little issues with self esteem. You want to be in the presence of women who love themselves, because then they are far more likely to love you!

While it may be painful to admit everyone is not going to be happy about the changes they see happening in you. You may lose some people along the way. But if your friends don't want to see you become a better person, are they truly your friends?

When a man wants you to change who you are then maybe he is not the man for you. Now think about this for a minute...if he wants you to change...does he really want someone else? Is he tolerating your weight or celebrating your voluptuous curves?

We have been tolerated for so long, we many times do not know how to respond to celebration. We so many times explain away a compliment.

In this chapter we will learn how to know the difference between TOLERATION and CELEBRATION. Recognize the difference and gauge your actions accordingly. Determine what is acceptable to YOU!

Now SISTAHGURLFRIEND, when your man tells you how absolutely drop dead gorgeous you look..DO NOT respond with, yeah but I am fat, or this is too tight, or my hair is not done, even a you really think so, is not acceptable.

There are two words I want to teach you in this chapter...the words are THANK YOU. When someone male or female compliments you....DO NOT, I repeat DO NOT apologize or explain it away! Now repeat after me...THANK YOU!

I also believe very strongly in Devine restitution. That which you give you receive threefold. Bearing this in mind, when you see a SISTAHGURLFRIEND who looks good; TELL her! Let her feel your adoration, or as the case may be the celebration, of her Good Hair Day! The funny thing about complimenting others...It makes YOU feel good!

Speak to those who only seem to tolerate you. Express your feelings without being confrontational. Ask them how they feel about being in your presence, how they feel about your success. Watch their body language and eyes. That is where the truth surely lies.

This chapter's assignment: Practice saying THANK YOU to compliments. Make THANK YOU a complete sentence, no comma. No further words are needed. Don't be at all surprised if you are uncomfortable when you don't put a comma in the *Thank You* sentence. After all, we have spent years explaining why others should not celebrate us.

Part two of this lesson is to practice sincerely complimenting others. You never know when a someone is having a VERY bad day, week, month, year or life. They may be in a relationship someone who only tolerates them and they haven't been celebrated in weeks, months or worse--ever! This is a win-win situation. You will make someone's day and you will feel wonderful having done so!

# Lesson Three (Now)

1. Do you wish to be treated differently in relationships?

2. What would you change?

3. Have you ever told these people their behavior is unacceptable?

4. Do your friends have pity parties and always invite you?

5. Do you participate?

6. Are your friends as (or more) successful as you?

7. When someone compliments you what is your response?

8. Do you compliment others when they look good?

# Notes

# Lesson Three (In 90 Days)

1. What, if anything, has changed in the way your close circle of people treat you?

2. What have you done to influence this change?

3. What happened when you confronted these people about the way they treated you?

4. In a relationship what happens when you are only tolerated?

5. Do you complain about what needs to change or set out to change it?

6. Are you getting involved with people with similar goals?

7. What's your response to compliments?

8. How do you feel when you compliment others?

# *Notes*

## *When Only the Very Best Will Do*

We spend so much of our time taking care of others. Giving others our all. We give and give and give until we give out and then of course, we give some more. Never taking enough for ourselves. There are so many others who need you. STOP IT!

Stop it right now! YOU need YOU! If you have ever flown on an airplane as the plane begins to taxi onto the run way for take off the flight attendants give you the safety instruction. These are the instructions to save your life. One of these instructions is if oxygen become necessary place the mask over your nose and mouth first!

Why do you think they tell us this? Because my SISTAHGURLFRIEND, if you don't help yourself first you will not be able to help anyone else.

This was the hardest of all the lessons for me to learn. How could I possibly give to myself first? What about my church, my husband, my children, my mother, my job, my friends? The list was endless.

Well chile, let me tell ya something. Other than God, this SISTAHGURLFRIEND comes first. It is for survival. These are the safety instructions to save my life. Once I started putting Parry first, I discovered that everyone got theirs.

An amazing thing happened once I started making myself my number one priority...I had more to give because there was no longer resentment. So many times when we are giving our all we are not happy about the situation. However, as in my case, I didn't know how not to give until it hurt.

As time passed and those around me saw that I was serious about taking care of myself first, I was astonished to find I had gained something else that was priceless... RESPECT.

Respect from those around me because they realized I was starting to love and take care of myself. I was no longer looking to others to supply my needs. I was no longer waiting to see what those around me were going to do for me because surely if they loved me they would see what I need and supply it – because that is what I would do for them! Yeah, right!

In the process of my divorce from Mr. Brown, he told me that he had always loved me in his own way. From deep inside my soul I looked him square in the eye and said, "I'm sorry, your way is not good enough anymore. For Mrs. Brown, only the very best will do!" He didn't understand. Chances are he still doesn't.

This chapter's lesson will be very difficult for most of us...and yes I still have to work on this one from time to time. You will have to make a choice between doing something for yourself or someone else. And you will choose YOU!

Now you must time this right! I am not suggesting that you pick a crucial thing that does need to be done immediately and say *"Oh no, I am going to the mall."* Evaluate the situation and determine if it is a need or want situation.

If it is truly a want situation, try this exercise. Little Johnny wants that new $50 designer jersey. There is $50 in the budget to spend on want shopping, but you really want that new lipstick you saw on your Sistahgurlfriend at church.

Now comes the hard part...buy the lipstick first and with what is left over go buy Johnny a nice shirt. Now if Johnny is not happy (which he will not be) because he didn't get the shirt he wanted...give him an option. Take this shirt or you will take it back and you will spend the rest of the money on YOU!

It is almost a given that Johnny will be upset at first, but better them than you. Over time Johnny will learn what he can expect from you. He will also learn that you love yourself enough to take good care of yourself without being selfish.

There s a delicate balance between healthy self love and selfishness. A healthy self love comes when you get your fair share of the love, time and money. Selfishness comes into play when we are getting way more than our fair share. For most of us who battle with self esteem issues, we will not have to worry about being selfish to a fault.

Confidence should never be confused with conceit. Healthy self esteem means you know you are all that, but not to the detriment of others. Conceit means you think that you are more than others.

# Lesson Four (Now)

1. Who do you spend most of your time taking care of?

2. List the people who demand you take care of them before you take of yourself?

3. What percentage of time do others spend taking care of you?

4. What percentage of time do you spend taking care of yourself?

5. List five things you do on a regular basis to pamper yourself.

6. Do you give yourself a monetary allowance just for things for YOU?

7. How do you feel about household appliance gifts for personal holidays?

8. Do you ever want to buy something for yourself but sacrifice for the *wants* of others?

# *Notes*

# *Lesson Four (In 90 Days)*

1.     How much time do you spend on yourself?

2.     Are there others that you take care of before yourself? Why?

3.     Do you wait for others to supply your needs? Explain.

4.     What percentage of time do you spend taking care of yourself?

5.     List five or more things you regularly to pamper yourself.

6.     Do you give yourself a monetary allowance just for things for you?

7.     Do you tell people what you would like to receive as gifts?

8.     Have you started shopping for yourself first?

# *Notes*

# *Know when to hold 'em.*
# *Know when to fold 'em!*

I enjoy playing cards for fun and for money. I have sashayed (as only a Diva can) up to the blackjack table with $40 and left with hundreds. On the other hand there have been times that I am just not lucky. I recognized what was happening, cut my loses and got up from the table.

Many of our relationships are like a card game. We need to recognize the game for what it is. Are you winning enough to feel that you are at least breaking even (getting out as much as you are putting in) or are you consistently placing bets and the house is building brand new mega casinos at your expense?

If there are people in your life that you consistently invest love, time and money, but never seem to get any return on your investment, then you need to cut your loses and move on. Everyone is not happy about your success or positive steps toward change. Each person in your life is not there to help you reach your goals, but to make sure that you aid them in their own quest for success (no matter how they measure success). We need to see them for what they are and act accordingly.

Now this is not telling anyone to leave your mate, stop talking to your siblings or tell your friends they are using you. What I am saying is look at your relationships, evaluate how much love, time and money you are investing. Then evaluate how much love, time and money you receive in return. This is not to say that this is a minute for minute, dollar for dollar evaluation. I once heard a minister when asking for an offering say it is not how much you give that matters, but how much you have left. In other words are you giving all that you can afford to give.

Are the people in your life giving all they can afford to give you? Is it enough to meet your needs. Remember, my ex-husband told me he loved me in his own way (gave all he could afford to give), I told him it wasn't good enough (he couldn't give enough to meet my needs).

For those people in your life that you wish to continue nurturing healthy relationships, talk to them, tell them you are trying to make some positive changes and will need their help. Explain that you will need their love and patience and they will see a new you emerging.

What you will see happen as you work on becoming a better you, they will either get with the program (embracing the new you) or they will move out of your way by choice or by omission.

The lesson for this chapter is to evaluate the relationships in your life. Are the people in your life loving and supportive? Here's an example: Your dream has always been to dance. Since the first time you saw Fame, you have wanted to take dance lessons. You think you are a natural, but someone you think loves you is telling you -- *you're too old!* Honey, look-a-here. If your skeletal and muscular system can withstand the stress then get out your leotard and tights and go for it!

Now on the other hand we need to have an open ear and mind to those who do have our best interest at heart. Those who want nothing but the best for us and gives us counsel out of love and concern. Many times we are not receptive to honest and loving criticism or the plain truth.

When your Sistahgurlfriend tells you that Tyrone is using you and you need to leave his unemployed, won't work in a pie factory butt, alone...you need to listen.

Know when to hold tight to those who will be of support and encouragement to you in your quest for the you, you want to become. On the other hand know when to begin to distance yourself from those who want to take more from you than they are willing or able to give.

# Lesson Five (Now)

1.      List people in your life that you do not like (even if you love them).

2.      List people who never seem to have anything to give to you.

3.      List people who you have a relationship with that is 60/40 or greater

4.      List people who are supporting you in all of your endeavors.

5.      List people who give you constructive and loving criticism

6.      List people who love you unconditionally.

7.      Are there dreams you have that are not being fulfilled because *friends* say you can't?

# *Notes*

# *Lesson Five (In 90 Days)*

1.    What are you doing to distance yourself from those you do not like?

2.    What are you requiring of those who never seem to have anything to give to you?

3.    In the relationships that are unbalanced, what are you doing to correct it?

4.    How do you express your appreciations for those who are constantly in your corner?

5.    Do you heed the advise of those who have your best interest at heart?

6.    Are you as receptive to loving yourself unconditionally as others are?

7.    What are you doing to realize your long delayed dreams.

# *Notes*

# *Permanent Solutions to Temporary Situations*

I sat in the kitchen of what anyone would consider a dream home with my friend Karen discussing the pros and cons of married versus single life. Karen being the expert on the married life and I on living single, she said that she so many times wonders why women will almost sell their souls to become *Mrs. Anybody.*

She is in the second decade of a marriage to her high school sweetheart and is very happy. They have two wonderful children who live in a house with spotless white carpet (I really want to know how she does it). As we sat there eating chicken gizzards with hot sauce my friend said something so profound I had to make it a chapter in this book.

Neither one of us could figure out why so many women are so bent on marriage (me being single via family court of the County of Los Angeles). She said so many women are looking for permanent solutions to temporary situations.

She went on to explain that a woman on the verge of bankruptcy will look for someone with good credit to help her finance her lifestyle. What she doesn't realize is that if she files bankruptcy her credit will be cleaned up in seven years. Will her marriage (a pseudo permanent solution) based on the wrong motivation (a temporary situation--bad credit) survive? What price will she have to pay for her new car, new home, shopping sprees at Bloomingdales? A price far beyond the value of a few dead Presidents is almost guaranteed.

Then there is my personal favorite: If I just have a baby he will commit for sure. Yes, he will commit – a disappearing act to be rivaled by David Copperfield.

What are we willing to compromise in order to get a quick fix for loneliness? Are we willing to put up with a man who only comes by when his needs are the motivation.

In my case my permanent solution was my marriage to a man who was the center of his own universe and invited me in when it suited him. He had shown me the attention I had so desperately needed. The temporary situation was low self-esteem. The price I paid was self respect.

Would you blindly make a purchase without knowing the cost? Of course you wouldn't (or shouldn't). The same must apply to our relationships. We must know the cost of the solution and believe me, nothing comes without a cost.

If you are looking for a man to take care of you so you don't have to work, know that he who pays the cost, truly is the boss. There are no two situations the same, therefore there is no way to say what the right solution is to any given situation. When in doubt re-read *"When Only the Very Best Will Do"*. You will find your solutions within you.

With this in mind, the lesson for this chapter is to make informed decisions. Don't make a commitment without considering all cost. If the cost seems too high, you should seriously consider declining the offer.

# *What's Sex Got to Do With It?*

I bet when you picked up this book you thought I was going to be telling you all about some bedroom action, huh? Well, surprise! To this point we have only discussed getting the love and attention you deserve. I discovered that being sexy is a result of little or nothing that goes on in the bedroom.

It is the attitude outside of the bedroom that is important. If you are confident and assured of the person you are (or aspiring to be) you will exude sexiness all over the place. When I polled a group of over 200 men (a tough job, but anything for my Sistahgurlfriends) 95% of them cited confidence as the single most attractive trait in a woman.

Some went so far as to say that a woman's size made no difference to them. It is the woman's attitude and healthy love for herself that commands their attention. It is the woman's flair that causes them to pause.

My mother was five feet tall (I think shorter) and weighed approximately three hundred and seventy-five pounds (or more because she would never tell us the truth about her weight or age). She was never without suitors. It was her warm smile, razor sharp wit and take me as I am or leave me the heck alone attitude that caused the men to all take notice.

There is nothing that you can put on (or take off) to make you sexy. Now there are fashions that can enhance your look. (Thinking back to that Christmas edition of the Frederick's catalog.) But it is not the clothes (or lack of clothes) that makes you sexy. Have you ever seen the same outfit on two people look totally different? On days when I am having a bad hair day, wearing a cap, leggings and a sweatshirt, I get as many, if not more adoring looks as when I am in an evening dress.

By expecting and only accepting love and respect your self esteem (the foundation of sexiness) will soar. It will be apparent in the way you walk, the way you talk, the way you smile, that you love you.

It is the aura and attitude that attracts the attention. Feeling good about who you are and loving yourself instills the confidence that attracts others to want to get to know the person that is loving the life she lives and living the life she loves.

Think back to the time when you really felt attractive, did others find you attractive, as well?

This chapter's lesson is to do what ever it takes to make yourself feel attractive. Adjust your attitude, get your hair done, take a bubble bath, workout. Getting the visual on this one?

Another important element in this exercise is to be receptive to compliments. Open yourself up to others to allow them to enjoy you. Remember those two little words we learned earlier in this book!

And....HAVE FUN!

# Lesson Six (Now)

1.  Rate your sexiness on a scale from 1 - 10. (1 being convent bound)

2.  When do you feel you sexy?

3.  Who makes you feel you sexy?

4.  What makes you feel sexy?

5.  Where (locale) do feel sexy?

6.  Do others find you sexy?

7.  How do you know others find you sexy?

8.  Name three thoughts you need to adjust to feel sexier.

# *Notes*

# Lesson Six (In 90 Days)

1.  Rate your sexiness on a scale from 1 - 10. (1 being convent bound)

2.  When do you feel you sexy?

3.  Who makes you feel you sexy?

4.  What makes you feel sexy?

5.  Where (locale) do feel sexy?

6.  Do others find you sexy?

7.  How do you know others find you sexy?

8.  Name three things you need to adjust to feel sexier.

# *Notes*

# *Smooth Sailing?*

NOT! When we have battled self esteem issues for most our lives it can be a daily struggle to stay on the positive side of things.

It is my hope that this book will serve as a motivator for those days when you just don't feel like feeling good. For whatever reason you are in a funk, allow yourself to feel it for a short while. Now that short while should not exceed any twenty-four hour period.

Get a support system. We've already talked about aligning ourselves with those who want to see us succeed. These are the same people who we want to use as our support system. We want to be able to call on Sistahgurlfriends when we are feeling just unnecessary. We want people who are up on most days and will extend a hand to pull us from any quagmire that has us captive.

A true Sistahgurlfriend will tell you the truth, even if you don't want to hear it. She will bring you to reality about any range of temporary situations. She may or may not give you advise, but she will always listen.

Make no mistake about it, you do not want to call on someone who is deeper in emotional despair than you are. Also understand that you do not always want to be the one who needs to be uplifted. In the *"Know When to*

*Hold 'em–Know When to Fold 'em"* chapter we discussed getting as much as you give, this applies to you as well. When a friend calls you, it normally means they want to talk. Don't be so quick to unload your burdens. When you pick up the phone be ready to listen.

When you dial be ready to talk. Don't expect for the person on the other end of the phone to just know you need to talk. And remember, you want to be the lifter more frequently than the liftee.

Loving and supporting one another is the strongest link in the SISTAHGURLFRIEND chain. Many times supporting only means listening. We are sometimes a little too hasty to give advise. On most occasions, even when we ask for the opinions of others we don't really want it. We just want to hear our problems out loud.

My favorite response to a SISTAHGURLFRIEND who is pouring her soul out to me is Gurl, I understand. That way she knows I am listening and really empathizing, but let's face it the decision is solely hers to make.

In this chapter's lesson we will recognize our dark day (notice the singular) and move past it as quickly as possible and then extend a hand to help a SISTAHGURLFRIEND out of her slump.

# *Lesson Seven (Now)*

1.  Who can you call upon when you are feeling depressed, unloved and just unnecessary?

2.  Are the people in your inner circle frequently depressed or unmotivated?

3.  How often do others call you to be lifted emotionally?

4.  How often do you call others to be lifted emotionally?

5.  When a friend calls you who starts talking first?

6.  Who can you call and always feel better when you hang up?

7.  Who's guaranteed to feel worse when you hang up?

8.  How often are you depressed?

# *Notes*

# *Lesson Seven (In 90 Days)*

1.  Who have you identified as your single most inspirational source of motivation?

2.  Are the people in your inner circle inspired and motivated?

3.  How often do others call you to be lifted emotionally?

4.  How often do you call others to be lifted emotionally?

5.  Are you a good listener?

6.  Do you recognize when you need motivation and call on those who can lift you up?

7.  How do you handle those who depress you?

8.  How do you move past your dark days?

# *Notes*

# *Is it Really Him?*

Time and time again you have ended up with someone who tolerates, rather than celebrates you. Why do they always use and abuse you? Why can't someone look inside and see what it is you need in order to make you happy? Why can't you find a Terry Winston? (A blatant plug for The Shirt Off His Back, ShanKrys Publishing $14.95.)

If you are consistently being chosen by the wrong men, then SISTAHGURLFRIEND you need to start being the chooser instead of the choosee. WHOA!! Am I saying you don't have to accept a man because he wants you? Yes, SISTAHGURLFRIEND, that is CORRECT! We tend to attract those who have issues, those who need fixing, those who have far more need-to-take than need-to-give.

If you constantly end up with someone who does not celebrate you, then it is time YOU take responsibility for your choices. No one can do any more to you than you allow them. So if Tyrone doesn't work, is not trying to work, blaming 'the man' because he can't find work, won't cook and clean while you work (you feeling me?) and you STILL support him, guess who's fault that is.

When I was having a very bad time in my marriage I realized if I had been my husband, I wouldn't have left me either! I provided a wonderful home, worked hard and took great care of our children, was a marvelous hostess and put up with his mess. I was so foolish to ask him at one time what would he do if I treated him with the same disrespect and disdain. Without hesitation he said he would leave me. Even at that, I stayed! I am not proud, actually quite the opposite, but there is real freedom in truth.

It took me more years (yes years) and counseling to understand I deserve only the best someone has to give to me. Once I came to that realization guess who got to steppin'?

Toleration indicates acceptance. If I tolerate your neglect or mistreatment, then I have sent a message that it is okay to continue doing just what you are doing.

It is so much easier to blame others for what is happening in our lives. It is less painful to say that Tyrone is no good and treats me like crap than to say why am I allowing Tyrone to treat me this way. The latter shifts the responsibility where it belongs, doesn't it?

*"No one can mistreat you without your consent."*
                                        *-Eleanor Roosevelt*

This not only applies to the men in your life obviously, but to all relationships. Family and those we consider friends will mistreat you if you allow them. It is up to you to take charge of your life. Take the responsibility for what you allow to happen to you and accept the consequences.

This chapter's lesson is a simple one...Look at how you have been treated in the past (or maybe even now). Accept responsibility for the good and the not so good. Remember, you deserve only the very best!

Now TAKE ACTION!!

# Lesson Eight (Now)

1.   When some mistreats you who do you blame?  Why?

# Notes

# Lesson Eight (In 90 Days)

1.　　Who is responsible for the treatment you receive?

# *Notes*

# *Fat is Not a Four Letter Word!*

Society has pounded (pardon the pun) into us that *fat* is a dirty word. It is not. It is an adjective, just like slim, skinny, plump, tall, short, etc. When a friend asked me one morning how I was, I responded *fat and sassy*, she was taken aback because I referred to myself as fat.

I am not ashamed that I am fat. I am in perfect health. I am a large woman who is physically fit and defy any 25 year old to compete with my energy level. (When this was written I had just turned 48.)

For so many years I tried to cover up my fat body because surely if I wore certain clothes a certain way no one could tell I was fat-*puhleeze*!

While shopping with my youngest daughter (who is honest to a fault) I stumbled upon an after five suit that was to die for. I looked wuuuuuuunderful in it, but it was a little tighter than I was used to wearing (back then). As I turned my body in every conceivable direction in the three way mirror in the dressing room, I asked the unthinkable –*Does my butt look big in this suit?* My daughter who never looked up from the teen music magazine she was reading to pass the time as I shopped, responded, *Mama, your butt is big.*

For the first time in my life someone had said that

to me without trying to intentionally hurt me. And that day in the discount clothing store that catered to large size women *I was set free*. I finally accepted the truth and it could no longer hurt me. My daughter without knowing it had taken the demons out of the words *my butt is big*.

My granddaughter (daughter of the same one who set me free) said to me one day as I struggled into a pair of control top pantyhose *Grandma your bones giggle*. (Apparently honesty is genetic.) Once I stopped laughing, I explained to this insightful five year old that no, grandma's bone can't giggle, but that Grandma is fat. My daughter was stunned by my reply.

I went on to explain to my daughter that as long as my granddaughter believed fat is a bad word then when one of her friends told her that her grandma is fat it could hurt her. But, now that I had taken the demons out of the word fat if someone told her that her grandma is fat, she would simply reply – *I know!*

We need to stop concentrating on what others say or think about us and focus on our inner self. When I stopped dieting and started living I lost 50 pounds. I started eating to live and working out to live longer. I am no longer consumed with the desire to be thin, because my self worth is not measured by the numbers on a scale and if it were – *I am worth my weight in gold.*

The weight loss industry grosses billions of dollars a year because we believe life is better in a size 6. No matter what size you are a 6, 16, 26, or 36. You are still you and unless you address your issues of self esteem, you will always be a victim of your own attitude.

I personally know a woman who is tall, long thick hair, size 5/6 (sometimes a 4) and is *never* happy. This same woman hates my size 24 (sometimes 26) butt because I am *always* happy. *Go figure!*

Our health is *most* important. Eat properly, drink lots of water (64 ounces per day minimum) and exercise. That is not telling you to rush out to join a gym. If I had all the money I have wasted on unused gym memberships, I would be taking my 100 closest friends to Las Vegas for the weekend. Get yourself a good pair of walking shoes, some head phones and start walking. It is great to have a walking companion, but don't wait for one. Start off slow, you will build momentum and stamina in no time. Your energy level will skyrocket and you will feel good about you because you are taking the time to take care of YOU!

The lesson for this chapter is to take the time to be healthy. Healthy attitudes and a healthy body is *the* winning combination!

# Lesson Nine (Now)

1. Do you look at your size as a negative attribute?

2. Are you most concerned about what you think or what others think about you?

3. Do you have healthy eating habits?

4. How many ounces of water do you drink each day?

5. Do you exercise? (Includes walking, dancing, etc.)

6. Do you know people who are thin and unhappy?

7. Do you know people who are fat and happy?

8. List adjective that describe your physical appearance.

# *Notes*

# Lesson Nine (In 90 Days)

1.      How do you view your size?


2.      Are you most concerned about what you think or what others think about you?


3.      Do you have healthy eating habits?


4.      How many ounces of water do you drink each day?


5.      Do you exercise? (Includes walking, dancing, etc.)


6.      How do you view people who are thin and still unhappy?


7.      How do you view people who are fat and happy anyway?


8.      List adjective that describe your physical appearance

# *Notes*

# *Personal Choices*

Rejection has to be one of the most painful of all feelings. When someone we love, or even are just attracted to, does not return those feelings we tend to turn the reasoning inward.

*He is not attracted to me because my breasts are too small. He doesn't love me because I am fat. She would be my friend if...*

When we take the blame for the personal preferences or choices of others we set ourselves up for rejection.

*Picture this.* A Ferrari is a sleek, lean, sexy machine, built for speed. The Ferrari is worth about $250,000. A Rolls Royce is a large, very plush machine built for comfort. The Rolls Royce is worth about $250,000.

Now, if you choose the Ferrari, that does not reduce the value of the Rolls. If you choose the Rolls, the value of the Ferrari remains the same. I can read your mind here. Parry has lost her mind she is talking about cars. No, I am talking about worth. Please understand, because someone's personal preference or choice may not include you for whatever reason, you must not take that as rejection. It is ***their*** preference.

I prefer younger men. I don't know why anymore than I know why my favorite color is black. It just is. When I am not attracted to a fine gentleman in my age group it does not mean that he is not a good choice for someone, just not me.

How many times have you looked at a man and did not find him attractive? So what makes you think that *every* man is going to look at you and say *"oh she is ALL THAT!"*

This is the same attitude we must take with ourselves. It never upsets me when a man isn't attracted to me, because he is exercising his right to choose.

As an avid Internet user, I have occasion to meet men on the Net. One evening I was feeling particularly spirited (with the help of Kendall Jackson) when a man asked me to describe myself, I used the following metaphor. *I am like a Sealy firm extra thick pillow top mattress. Now you can choose to sleep on the mattress or a box spring, it is up to you.*

Once he stopped laughing we struck up a friendship that is still very active. He was intrigued by the way I value myself (my self worth). We have not become romantically involved because he is too old for me and I am not the body type he desires, but it has not changed our worth to each other, but more importantly ourselves!

Your lesson for this chapter is to STOP confusing the personal preferences of others with rejection. Determine your own self worth and understand that only you can change your value. Do not expect to wake up tomorrow morning and feel that you have this all under control and you will never feel rejected again. This like all of the lessons in this book take time to get into our spirit. Practice, daily, the exercises outlined here and one day when a man you have set your sights for doesn't even acknowledge that you breathe that you will be able to shrug your shoulders and say, *His loss*, and mean it.

# Lesson Ten (Now)

1.    When a man is not attracted to you, what is your first reaction?

2.    How do you feel about him?

3.    How do you feel about you?

# *Notes*

# Lesson Ten (In 90 Days)

1.      Is personal preference confused with rejection?


2.      How do you feel when someone *prefers* someone different?


3.      How do you feel about you?

# *Notes*

# *Taking Your Show On the Road*

Now that we have worked on our attitudes and the way we view ourselves and others, there are bound to be some outward manifestations of the new you!

There are so many myths and misconceptions about women of size and what they should or should not wear. First and foremost, if you have a full length mirror, use it! If you don't, get one! And remember it does not lie. If that mirror says you don't look quite as well put together as you should; then you don't! If you have children (no matter what the age, 4 - 54) they are painfully honest, ask them how you look. But be prepared for what they really think!

The first item on the Fashion Do's & Don'ts is a result of an encounter I had in my very first seminar. There was a young woman in the work shop who was very obviously suffering from low self esteem. She would not make eye contact with me and toward the end of the workshop raised her hand and asked my opinion about wearing red.

She and I were about the same skin tone. She said she loved bright colors, especially red, but had been told she was too dark. I shared the story of how I met a previous boyfriend in the mall when he spotted me on the first level from the third level because I was wearing a red jacket.

I returned to the same forum the following year. As I finished a book signing at the end of the of the session, a very stylish woman stood before me and asked if I remembered her. Her face looked familiar, but I was clueless. She told me the question she had asked me the year before and I instantly knew, though she looked totally different.

She looked taller, appeared to have lost weight (though it may have just been that she now stood erect), make-up was flawless and she was wearing an absolutely gorgeous designer suit – and yes it was red!

### *Fashion Gospel According EbonySatin*

- Red is an attention getter and compliments *every* skin tone! If you like red (orange, sunshine yellow or lime green), wear it!
- Classic black is very flattering, but you are the same size in a black dress as you are in a green one. Wear black because you like it, not because it is slimming.
- Loose clothes do not make you look slimmer.
- Do not squeeze your size 18 self into a 14 and think you look cute.
- Short skirts can be worn at any age.
- Polyester is not your friend.
- Your arms are the same size with or without

sleeves.
- Your buttocks are the same size whether you wear your shirt tucked in or not.
- Your face is the same size no matter your hair length.
- If you have a waist (and everyone does – *it is that area between your bust and your hips*) you can wear belts.
- Jeans and leggings *are* available in your size
- Never ever step out of your house in rollers, house shoes or a bathrobe!
- Spend the time and money to get a massage monthly. If you are on a tight budget contact a massage school.
- Treat yourself to a facial.
- Arch your eyebrows.
- Get a manicure and pedicure regularly.
- Always leave home like you may run into the man of your dreams...you just might!
- Wear make up to enhance your natural beauty, war paint is used for battle.
- Wear sexy DIVA make-em-fall-to-their-knees-and-say-please shoes. The heel of a shoe *does* enhance the shape of your legs. There are some serious *divalicious* low heel shoes, too!
- Spend a couple extra dollars...buy ultra sheer panty hose. (*Re-read When Only the Very Best Will do.*)
- Wear sexy underwear. Oh I can read your mind...*but who will know.* YOU WILL!!!

These are just a few suggestions to enhance that new attitude you are sporting. It is so much fun to dress to impress.

The clothes don't make you a DIVA...they show just how DIVAish you are!

# *Lesson Eleven (Now)*

1.      Do you own and use your full length mirror.

2.      Are there colors you shy away from because they draw attention?

3.      Do you have an all black wardrobe?

4.      Do you have several different sizes of clothes in your closet?

5.      Do you hide your arms, knees, buttocks, etc?

6.      Do wear clothes that show or hide your body?

7.      Do you take the time to make sure you are always looking your best?

8.      Would your mother be proud of your underwear if you were in an accident?

# *Notes*

# *Lesson Eleven (In 90 Days)*

1.  Do you check your mirror **every time** before leaving your home?

2.  What colors do you wear to attract attention?

3.  Does your wardrobe contain a wide variety of colors?

4.  Do you expose your arms and knees or tuck in your shirt?

5.  Have you donated those size 8's to charity?

6.  Do wear clothes that show or hide your body?

7.  Do you take the time to make sure you are always looking your best?

8.  Would your mother be proud of your underwear if you were in an accident?

# *Notes*

# *Doing It and Doing It Well*

Changing of attitudes is a gradual and life long process. We start today and don't stop until we die. Hopefully we will be growing and changing for the better until we move on to another plane.

We must practice and practice and then practice some more the life lessons that are to afford us change. Even after we have done some life changing things for months or even years, it takes so little to backslide.

By aligning ourselves with those who want to see us succeed and being a lifter more than a liftee, we will stay strong. Don't be surprised when others try to test you. They will test to see if you are serious or if this is just a phase. It may not even be intentional, but remember those around us are comfortable with the way we use to be.

Gradually you will notice subtle changes. You will step a little lighter, sway your hips a little more, tolerate a little less mess, smile a little brighter for no reason other than you are happy being alive!

Like the pianist who plays Carnegie Hall, so are we challenged to continue to sharpen our skills. The skills it takes to become the woman that you want to be! A DIVA (like me) makes it look so easy...and perhaps for some it comes natural, but this DIVA has worked long and hard to become a self assured (on most days) confident woman who knows she is sexy whether she is stretching the seams on her size 24 suit or stepping out in a perfect size 16 sequined cut to the navel, split to the waist evening dress.

If this task was easy, everyone would be doing it. It takes a woman who is committed to change. One who wants to get ALL that life has to offer and is willing to work for it

The final lesson is to put into practice what you have learned in this little book. Remember in the beginning I told you to take what you can use and discount the rest. Perhaps all of this applies to you or maybe none of it does. I am willing to guarantee that you know at least one someone this will help. I only humbly ask that you simply pass it on.

# Lesson Twelve (Now)

1. Are you worthy to be loved just the way you are?

2. How do you prove that to yourself daily?

3. Who do you look to for love?

4. Are you afraid to tell people what you really think in fear they won't still love you?

5. Are you afraid to say NO?

6. Do you stay in relationships because they are familiar or comfortable?

7. Are you afraid of success?

8. Are you willing to make the commitment required to make some positive changes?

# *Notes*

# *Lesson Twelve (In 90 Days)*

1.	Are you worthy to be loved just the way you are?

2.	How have you proven that to yourself?

3.	Who do you look to for love?

4.	When you tell people what you really think, do they still love you?

5.	What happens when you say NO?

6.	Have you made any decisions about unhealthy relationships?

7.	How do you measure success towards a healthy mental and emotional state?

8.	What changes have you made since you first read *Sexy Doesn't Have a Dress Size*?

# *Notes*

# *When It is All Said and Done...*

...will it be what you've said you were going to do or what you have done to change your life? We so many times talk about the things we want to change in our lives, but with this little book, I want to challenge you into action.

Look inside of yourself, find the things that you want to change and set a plan of action. Then learn to cherish the things you wouldn't dare change. Encourage your SISTAHGURLFRIENDS to do the same.

Thank you so much for allowing me to share my life experiences with you. My prayer is that something that was said on these pages will help you to become all the YOU, you want to be.

# *About the Author*

Parry 'EbonySatin' Brown is a motivational speaker committed to making a difference in the lives of people everywhere. Her *Sexy Doesn't Have a Dress Size* seminar has packed the house from coast to coast. She is the author of the number one best seller *The Shirt Off His Back* (ShanKrys Publishing $14.95) which is being re-released by Random House Publishing in early 2001.

In the seminars some of us cry, others laugh, but we all identify with the struggle it takes to sustain a healthy self love. For seminar booking information please call (310) 213-2515.

Parry is a happily divorced mother of two and grandmother of two. She was born in Wilmington, North Carolina, grew up in Baltimore, Maryland and has lived in the greater Los Angeles area since the early 70's.

_Parry 'EbonySatin' Brown_

## Order Information

### Sexy Doesn't Have a Dress Size Gear
☐ Cap ($13)    ☐ T-Shirt ($20)   ☐ Sweat Shirt ($35)

### Books
_____ Sexy Doesn't Have a Dress Size ($9.95 ea)
_____ Sexy Doesn't Have a Dress Size CD ($14.95 ea)

Merchandise: $ _____

Shipping/Handling \_\_\_\_\_5.00\_

Total this order $_____

Name:_____

Addr: _____

City: _____ ST \_\_\_\_\_ Zip _____

Daytime Phone: (\_\_\_\_) _____ Fax _____

E-Mail: _____

Make Checks Payable to:
**ShanKrys Publishing, Inc.**
Fax to: (310) 514-1399  with this form

Or mail to:
1525 Aviation Blvd. Ste A106
Redondo Beach, CA 90278-2800